Forty Days of Prayer Journal

Volume 1

Sandy Gleespen

Outskirts Press, Inc.
Denver, Colorado

The opinions expressed in this manuscript are solely the opinions of the author and do not represent the opinions or thoughts of the publisher. The author has represented and warranted full ownership and/or legal right to publish all the materials in this book.

Forty Days of Prayer Journal
Volume 1
All Rights Reserved.
Copyright © 2009 Sandy Gleespen
V3.0

This book may not be reproduced, transmitted, or stored in whole or in part by any means, including graphic, electronic, or mechanical without the express written consent of the publisher except in the case of brief quotations embodied in critical articles and reviews.

Outskirts Press, Inc.
http://www.outskirtspress.com

ISBN: 978-1-4327-3036-9

Outskirts Press and the "OP" logo are trademarks belonging to Outskirts Press, Inc.

PRINTED IN THE UNITED STATES OF AMERICA

Introduction

We all want to touch the hand of God. We want to see our lives improve. We want to develop the focus and effectiveness of our prayer life. It is the beginning that is difficult.

First, there are all the layers of lies that have bombarded our thinking. They constantly taunt us that God is either too big and powerful to hear or even care, or He is watching us every minute in hopes of catching us failing again. In reality, He is our Creator, Advocate, Champion and much, much more. He just wants us to take the time to get to know Him. He continually loves us first.

Then, there are all the forces of life and hell that attempt to steal every minute of our days. There are not enough quiet moments to get personal with God. Quality time is preserved by consistently taking some time every day. Like a seed planted and cared for with water and light and time, our spiritual life grows and blooms and makes new fruitful seeds every season.

This little book is a tool to use on your attempt to head closer to the outstretched finger that the Almighty has waiting for you. Like a little child reaching up for Daddy's thumb, we can skip with a new stride on life's journey when we are in step with Our Heavenly Father.

The daily prayers are short, but meant to launch you to your own meditations. They bring reference to Scripture, but are only a springboard to your personal seeking of the Word of Truth. Grab a few minutes here or ponder throughout the day, but carve out your portion of time to discover your unique relationship and fresh layers of our God who is the Great I AM.

Prayers #1 Your Mercy

We pray for Your Mercy, O God. I must humble myself and pray and seek Your face. To humble myself requires confessing my sins, not the sins of my neighbor or enemy, but my sins. I must compare my life to Your holiness, not just looking around to see if my actions are equal or better than the next guy's. Then You have promised to heal our land.

Please give us leaders that are better than we deserve, that is mercy. Please help us to act in obedience to Your will and plans and laws; that will bring order and peace. Please help us to remember that the two greatest commandments are to love You with all our heart and soul and mind and strength; and to love other people as You want me to love myself.

I thank You for all the opportunities that You put in my path today. Help me to ask You for Wisdom when they come my way. Help me to be obedient to the answers You give me.

Amen.

My verse for today:

_____

_____

_____

My prayer:

_____

_____

_____

_____

_____

_____

_____

Prayers #2 Your Pathway

Where can I go from Your Spirit? Please lead me to the pathways that will be exactly what I need to prepare me for tomorrow. You are my source and my strength. I do not fear.

I cannot find joy in anything unless the center of my focus is You. Without Your presence of love and peace and goodness, all my efforts are selfish and meaningless. All of my best intensions will come to fruitless gain, chaff in the wind, without godly purpose.

Please strengthen those who fight for our freedoms. Please pour out your Wisdom and Knowledge for those making the big decisions as to how our country is to proceed. We will keep asking for Your mercy. Do not give us what we deserve, but teach us as Our Father. We come to You as a child who comes for help. Abba, Father, Daddy God! Please show us Your pathway.

Amen.

My verse for today:

_____

_____

_____

My prayer:

_____

_____

_____

_____

_____

_____

_____

Prayers #3 Your Perfect Law

Help me to remember that You are the Lord my God, and You brought me out of bondage. I may have no other gods before me. Please show me the other gods in my life. Help me to surrender all of them to You. Help me to see clearly that when I fail to give You everything, life makes no sense at all.

Thank You for giving me boundaries with purpose. Help me to realize that the laws are not for Your sake, but for mine. There are reasons, that benefit me, for following You, for working on obedience. The spirit of the law covers every situation. You show me in my conscience right from wrong. Forgive me, again and again, for all the times I have chosen wrong.

Let me be a reflection of goodness and kindness and obedience. Help me to practice patience with people who bother me. Please teach me a better way to apply Your Perfect Law today. Help me to remember to thank You for Your solutions.

Amen.

My verse for today:

_____

_____

_____

My prayer:

_____

_____

_____

_____

_____

_____

_____

Prayers #4 Your Outstretched Hand

Thank you, O Lord, for showing me what love really means. Please remind me that love is patient and kind and does not seek its own way. Help me remember that You offer your outstretched hand to me in not only the huge redemptive ways, but also the day-to-day helping me find my keys ways, too.

Please help me to receive enough forgiveness from You, for all my faults and wrongdoings, to have enough left over to give to those who I feel have hurt me. I know that I do not have the ingredients in myself to make forgiveness. I need to confess my sins to You, and only then will I be handed enough forgiveness to pass around.

I praise You for giving me sunrises and sunsets, for mountains and seashores, for the amber waves of grain. I choose to trust that You will keep me in the palm of Your hand and never leave me, even when I go off in my own dark way. Help me live Your kind of love today.

Amen.

My verse for today:

_____

_____

_____

My prayer:

_____

_____

_____

_____

_____

_____

Prayers #5 Your Walk of Forgiveness

Dear Father God, please help me to remember that Your forgiveness is a special gift. You do not give me my just do, but offer me better than I deserve. Please help me to be thankful in every circumstance, that all is working for my good. You turn everything around when I confess my guilt. Help me to never fear honestly admitting my wrong part. I need Your assurance to confess, knowing that You have already paid the price for my forgiveness...Your only begotten Son.

I want to start each day happy to know that You are always ready to listen to my cries. Help me to offer praise and thanksgiving along with my prayers for things I think I want or need. Help me to trust that You really want the very best for me, even when the pathway takes me through some rocky spots, causing me to hurt or even bleed.

Open my eyes to look for someone that needs to experience Your forgiveness today. Help me to look up from all my busy-ness to take the time to listen and point the way to cleansing steps. You will help me to have something to say that will brighten an otherwise cloudy day and offer hope. Help me to do that, please!

Amen.

My verse for today:

_____

_____

_____

My prayer:

_____

_____

_____

_____

_____

_____

Prayers #6 Your Vision

You led Moses up a mountain to receive the law from Your very hand. I cannot grasp what that was like. Help me to catch the vision of Your Glory. Help me to let Your Holy Spirit write Your law upon my heart. Help me to love Your ways as David did. I am asking that Your law will transform my life, my being.

You said that if we are humble and pray, You would heal our land. Show us, as a nation, how to be humble; teach us to pray with more than meaningless words. Show us how to put others ahead of ourselves. Show us how to be transparent when we come boldly to Your throne of grace. Strip away the layers of self-righteousness with which we have attempted to cover our spiritual poverty.

Let the joy of the Lord be my strength today. Help me to choose to look at the good in people and in situations that surround my day. Help me to reflect the love You have showered on me to someone that feels unloved and alone. Help me to travel the pathway that You have put before me today with the understanding that You are supplying all my needs and have given good gifts to me, Your child.

Amen.

My verse for today:

_____

_____

_____

My prayer:

_____

_____

_____

_____

_____

_____

_____

Prayers #7 Your Prayer Point

I was reading about the Mercy Seat. Only those with a willing heart could give for its making. Please give me a willing heart. I confess that my heart is selfish and centered on things that concern me, my family and those closest to me. Help me to see beyond that tight circle. Help me to have compassion on the weakest, without offering the substitute of pity for love. Remind me that pity requires a downward spiral to feed its greedy need for failure. Love always lifts up and gives hope, and offers a way of escape.

Teach me something new about serving You in spirit and in truth...TODAY! Help me to pick up my manna every morning without trying to hold enough over so I do not need to talk to You the next day. Clear away the thoughts of <u>having</u> to spend time in prayer and replace those falsehoods with the reality that I am offered the privilege to be refreshed and renewed and enlightened with Your Way and Truth and Life!

I ask You to begin a circle of prayer friends that surround those who lead us and have put themselves in harms ways to defend our freedoms. Please, O Lord, shower Your comfort, Your peace, Your Wisdom, Your protection, Your anointing... Help us to pray effectively as the need comes to mind.

Amen.

My verse for today:

_____

_____

_____

My prayer:

_____

_____

_____

_____

_____

_____

Prayers #8 Your Mission

Thank You for showing us the patterns and principles of life. Why is it so difficult to just believe that You know best and follow? My heart is self-contained. I want to be in control of my small world. What is amazing is that the more I surrender, the more You give back for me to manage.

There are hurting people all around us screaming for someone to fix their lives. Some hurt so deeply that they are now silent and have given up even asking. How do I help? How can I make a difference? It is not so much by addressing the crowds, but by reaching out a hand to one person at a time. Help me, that I will keep from being too busy to love with Your kind of selfless compassion.

I pray for a blanket of joy today! As I cover myself with the awareness that You offer me good gifts and a happy ending, I really have more to share. Pick me up off my couch of contentment and set me in the middle of a world of stone-cold figures. Please let me engage fully in my piece of Your mission. It is really about You connecting to each and every person that fits into this puzzle of life. Help me to "get it".

Amen.

My verse for today:

_____

_____

_____

My prayer:

_____

_____

_____

_____

_____

_____

_____

Prayers #9 Your Holiness

I need to come to You...when I feel weak and need You to carry me; when I am happy and no one else knows the depths of why; when I am confused and need You to sort the truth from the lies and make it all clear; when I am proud of a job well done and do not want to brag about it to another person (I need to tell You thanks for enabling me to complete the job); when someone hurts me to the core and You understand and always show me why the hurts inside of them spilled over on to me.

Someday, when I get to know You (even as I have been known by You), I am sure that my hope will melt into Truth. Teach me the different shades of Your Holiness. The White Light of Holiness becomes the spectrum of the rainbow of Your character when You shine on me. The prisms of my tears and pain reflect who You are to the world that goes through the mud of life without seeing that it can all work for good. Clean my mirror today.

Thank You, thank You, thank You to the Triune God!! Your Word is a light that keeps me safe. The darkness cannot hide from You. Your thoughts are too wonderful for Me. Your ways are not my ways and Your thoughts are not my thoughts. Help me to explore the height, the depths, the breadth of Your creation and be in awe!

Amen.

My verse for today:

_____

_____

_____

My prayer:

_____

_____

_____

_____

_____

_____

Prayers #10 Your Family Plan

Dearest Lord, God Almighty! Thank you for helping me make it through another day. Sometimes I rush around and do not think that I have time to stop and pray. But then I realize that I do not have enough time to miss coming to You for direction and strength and hope and Wisdom. When I attempt to run my household on my own, I only miss the mark.

I appreciate family. There I find lessons in how to love on every level. From the innocent baby to the aging parent, we learn to give not because of the return, but for the simple joy of touching one who knows us best. Then there is the sister-love! We think or feel or act so much alike that love flows effortlessly. And best of all comes when a husband-lover chooses to forget the flaws and shouts our best parts for the entire world to hear!

Family was designed to point the way to Father-God, Holy Spirit and Jesus the Son. You let me be part of this perfect family. You call me Your child, Your friend, Your witness. Help me to prefer the love and truth of family to the calling of cheap substitutes that leave me wanting more and more. Show me how to be a better part of Your family and mine.

Amen.

My verse for today:

_____

_____

_____

My prayer:

_____

_____

_____

_____

_____

_____

Prayers #11 Your Majesty

You wake me with the morning light! I love each sunrise and sunset, the rainbow of colors reminding me that You shine over my day and keep me safe at night. The majestic mountaintops let me know that my journey has just begun; I know just a speck of dust of who You are. The rushing rivers sing songs of bubbling joy at surrendering to the pathway of Your choosing. The silence of a forest speaks of Your strength, the cycle of birth and death and starting a new sprig of life again.

I ask that my purpose in this symphony of creation will be clear enough to give me hope today. Help me to be motivated by Your still small voice that calls from deep in my inner-most being. Move me to do and not just dream about what I am to accomplish this day. Surprise me with a job that is rewarding and exciting and attainable!

When I speak to those in my path, please help me to find a point of common ground. Lead me in my conversations. Let my non-verbal messages be of acceptance and encouragement; these shout so much louder than any mere words. Help me to look into each soul and feel needs and hurts, so that I care enough to offer up a prayer that plants a seed.

Amen.

My verse for today:

_____

_____

_____

My prayer:

_____

_____

_____

_____

_____

_____

Prayers #12 Your Word

Thank You for the Words hidden in my heart! When I drive down the road, when I work at my desk, when I load the washer, when I clean the dirty dishes, when I work out in the yard...I have a storehouse of Truth to balance out the blast of lies that are thrown my way every day. Help me to choose to remember the Truth, even when it shines the light on my closet sins. Help me to trust that You have already forgiven me, and my job is to confess and repent.

Help me to begin at the "In the beginning..." and go straight through to the "...be with you all. Amen." I hear the bits and pieces at church, but I need to fill in the gaps and get it all to see the whole Truth and nothing but. To be a witness, I need to see every part and immerse myself into the world that is more solid than when I knock on wood.

Help me to enjoy the history and the model made of heaven. Let me offer praise and pour out my woes when I feel alone. Lead me to discover the mysteries and deep cryptic messages written by prophetic hands. Give me the eyes of a child who sees the characters act out the wonder for the first time. Teach me the order of the Body of the Christ (who came all the way to earth to bridge the gap).

Amen.

My verse for today:

_____

_____

_____

My prayer:

_____

_____

_____

_____

_____

_____

_____

Prayers #13 Your Walk of Obedience

Dear Lord, please help me through transition times. We tend to be comfortable when deep into our routines. A safe flow of people, places and things that look and feel familiar bring us peace. But it is really You. Even through the wilderness and when traveling in tents, if we can keep from grumbling, if we can remember to follow Your directions closely, life's ebbs and flows will be interesting and rewarding.

Obedience is more important than looking spiritual. Sometime I have to sacrifice my image for taking time to answer a cry for help. Help me to search my heart for the motives of my giving. Help me to seek to please You more than other people. When I want to shine, please take the spotlight and show the crowd that Your love is waiting in the wings to be more than a someday Savior.

Help me to be Your hands, feet, listening ears to someone that feels life is a fun-house and they are struggling through the passageways, just barely holding up. Thank You that my past pains have been washed away to reveal spiritual nuggets of truth and hope. I am so glad that when we give our hardships to You, the memories hold lessons and not bitterness. Keep me safe today from temptations that will try to replace the calm in the midst of any storm.

Amen.

My verse for today:

_____

_____

_____

My prayer:

_____

_____

_____

_____

_____

_____

_____

Prayers #14 Your Healing

Good morning, Lord! Thank You for putting my messes together again. When I fall off the wall and crack my perfectly positioned facade, You remind me that the inside is what counts. You always see my inside...and love me anyway. Help me to be transparent before Your throne, when I come to ask or confess or to sit and be comforted. Help me to have enough faith in Your love to be honest with both You and myself.

I ask for healing. There are those whose wounds are inside, some outside and some are just spinning from the constant battering. Please work the same kind of healing miracles that You did when you told the man to pick up his mat. You didn't go on strike. You didn't lose Your power. You are able to heal and forgive and mend the broken hearted. Please show me how to pray for someone today who is ripe for an answer.

When Your answers are not my answers, please help me to adjust. Please help me to find the hidden joy in taking the longest route to the finish line. Please help me to stop to chat with people going my way, too. And when all is done, please help me to strengthen the one just starting down the path.

Amen.

My verse for today:

_____

_____

_____

My prayer:

_____

_____

_____

_____

_____

_____

Prayers #15 Your Purpose

Sometimes I have to see the ugly parts of my life, and life in general, to understand You better. I am really better for having been broken and healed and comforted by Your Holy Spirit than to never have known pain at all. The athlete cannot reach new heights or speeds without pushing to the point of pain. My child will not learn to stop until she skins her knee, more than once.

Please open my eyes to the kinds of pain that I can mend. Please help me to focus on the wrongs that I can actually right. Please help me to be more effective in my crusades, not wasting time running around stonewalls that are not meant for me to crush. Give me my marching orders and help me focus there, not on my brother's duties. Remind me to come to You for my daily list of things that I must do.

I trust You for giving me room to fail. I trust You for letting my adversary make his own choices. I believe in Your power to turn every single evil plan into something that will benefit the Kingdom of God. Help me to remember that Jesus did not have the biggest house or the best job or even the prettiest wife and cleverest children. He knew it was about more than just here. He understood that the road to resurrection comes through death. Teach me to die to my ways and plans so that I may rise to new heights.

Amen.

My verse for today:

_____

_____

_____

My prayer:

_____

_____

_____

_____

_____

_____

_____

Prayers #16 Your Servant

Please send Your hand to cover the leaders of our nation and those who are on their way to lead. I pray for selfless service to be the goal. I pray that those who push for power and misdirected gain will be exposed and halted in their tracks. I pray for servants to rise and answer the call to give life and limb, to turn godless tides to You.

Help me to see a way that I can give my time and spirit to better the community in which I walk and shop and go to church. Help me to see opportunities to care for one person here and another there, all adding up to make a difference. Remind me of how You gave Yourself to heal and touch, then went up to a mountain to pray, only to return again to love and offer the arrow of truth to point the way.

Forgive me for the numerous times I crossed to the other side of the road to avoid a hand in need. Forgive me for how often I make excuses for ignoring that still small voice prompting me to make a call or visit someone who is hurting and urgently needs for me to pray. Help me to act next time and not go my own way.

Amen.

My verse for today:

_____

_____

_____

My prayer:

_____

_____

_____

_____

_____

_____

_____

Prayers #17 Your Strength

When I am tired or lonely or pressed with life's problems, You are forever my comfort and strength. When I look around and wonder why the world embraces false principles and meaningless goals, You stabilize my thinking. Please remind me that I am responsible for coming to You and confessing my need, and my sins. If I do that, You will adjust the rest.

We are told: The joy of the Lord is my strength. How do I return to the joy of my salvation? Return to the simple pleasures of first love. Embrace the moments of sitting through a sunset. Count the different colors of nature and marvel at the Creator of them all. Sit beside the still waters and believe that death is but a shadow. Look for signs that God is real and just and loving and close at hand. Choose to take one tiny step of obedience after another, until a habit is formed.

When I let You, my life is transformed in the simple pleasures of Your nature, Your character, Your vision of life. Turn my head around. Stop me in my tracks. Give me a time-out to think about putting things back in order. Search me, O God, and know my heart. Try me and know my thoughts. Lead me in Your way...everlasting!

Amen.

My verse for today:

_____

_____

_____

My prayer:

_____

_____

_____

_____

_____

_____

Prayers #18 Your Creativity

Thank you for reminding me that You anointed the workers and artists, by the power of Your Holy Spirit, to build the temple. Help me enjoy the creativity, the labor, the calling in which I will find my true self. Your plan for me is completely unique. My vision has a personal comfort that is a light yoke and no burden. Why have I bound myself in others' expectations? Why have I stifled the flow of creativity in fear of rejection or belittling remarks? I confess my fears and failures.

As You lead me to go the extra mile, I will see views that I would otherwise miss. Move me to put in the time. Remind me to offer the glory and praise to You, and not to sink into the mire of my own adulation. There is such a fine line between pride and praise. Only by depending completely on that anointed power of Your Holy Spirit can I possibly balance on the wire of success without teetering between condemnable inaction and arrogant accomplishment.

Holy Spirit, You are my Comfort and my Pillar of Strength! I need to depend on You to keep me balanced though life. Free me to become more than I can imagine. Expose the lies of mediocrity that keep me molded into a less-than-perfect pattern cut from worn-out paper. Expose the lies that pull me away from my purpose to live each day I have remaining on this earth. Show me my next step.

Amen.

My verse for today:

_____

_____

_____

My prayer:

_____

_____

_____

_____

_____

_____

_____

Prayers #19 Your Testing

How do You keep Your cool with all these disobedient children? We are constantly testing You. You tell us to do this or do not do that, but we go flippantly along on our way to a cliff of destruction. For those points of no return, You have scribed that such action will lead to death. Too harsh, we cry! But it is true. Sin will lead to death. We need to take the warnings and the laws to heart. This is serious stuff.

Please shine Your light of Truth on the places in my life that are leading me to self-annihilation. I am blinded by my efforts to keep myself clean and pure. There is no hope of that. Only the "whosoever will come" to the Son is washed whiter than snow. Then it is Your call, not mine. Then it is all of me, not my stingy morsel. Only at the point of total surrender do You give me back the freedom to live and move and discover my being.

Thank You for giving me more than 70 times 70 times to turn back to say I'm sorry. It helps so much to know without a doubt that I have been forgiven before I come. If I had to face an angry, unrelenting god, I would cringe in fear and never come. You open Father-arms and let the child in me jump into Your lap of love. Abba, Father, Daddy-God, please forgive my selfish, centered ways that take me into disobedience. I love that I can always come running back to You!

Amen.

My verse for today:

_____

_____

_____

My prayer:

_____

_____

_____

_____

_____

_____

Prayers #20 Your Hope

Thank you for hope that good things are coming. Help me to be looking for Your best when I am disappointed that I did not get my way. Let me really see the truth that Your love for me is bigger than I could imagine. You know my unruly hairs and my every word that should not be uttered. You understand my thoughts and dreams and plans and want my success to be such that it will not destroy me in the process. Help me to offer my good gifts to You as readily as I throw my thrash for You to fix.

When I am with someone that does not have what I do, please help me to know how to lend a hand. Please help me to really listen to the underlying hurt and not just skim over the symptoms because I can't be bothered. Please help me to understand compassion, not as a tool to enslave, but as an instrument that lifts from swamps and makes the impossible happen. Help me lend a hoping hand.

I need You to show me my perfect steps today. Some days, like this, I do not know where to begin. You comfort me when I am scattered. You excite me when I am blah. You direct me when I am running around in circles. I am coming to You today for all of that and more. Only You know just what is best for me to do today, how best to spend my minutes and hours. I want Your priorities, because mine do not always make sense. I love that You are not bothered, but actually like it when I keep asking, "What's next?"

Amen!

My verse for today:

_____

_____

_____

My prayer:

_____

_____

_____

_____

_____

_____

_____

Prayers #21 Your Relationships

You are the lover of my soul! Thank You for giving me a rock on which to stand when life rushes by like a river in a flood. You do send help in many forms. You do encourage me through the many outstretched arms of flowing care. Please teach me that when I think I hear You wrong, that Your ways are higher than my ways. Your plans are bigger than my plans. Your purposes reach out for relationships more than for awards.

Thank you for the people in my life. Thank you for family. Thank you for my best friend and lover. Thank you for new friends and friends that go back to when life was young and we played together. Thank you for the people that are touched by the people that I touch. Help me to be the one that touches someone enough that they look hard to find if You are really there.

Give me a new vision for tomorrow. When things take a turn that I didn't expect, please show me the way down the new road. Give me an expectant heart that builds on the experiences I have passed through in preparation for the next assignment. You use every lesson to help me pass the next test. Thank You for the assurance that Your plan for me is perfect and exciting and manageable.

Amen.

My verse for today:

_____

_____

_____

My prayer:

_____

_____

_____

_____

_____

_____

Prayers #22 Your Miracles

You make me lie down in green pastures and lead me beside still waters. I pray that You will be the refresher of my soul. I look forward to holding Your hand and jumping over logs and crushing fallen leaves. Thank Your for the change of seasons, in nature and in my life.

Bring me back to simple times. Help me hold tightly to yes and no. Teach me to believe Your Word is true and I can really seek out answers for my life in pages penned so long ago. When life is very gray, help me turn to the black and white and red. Help me do more than talking, and even writing, about praying for people that I love; help me do it every day when I drive or wash the dishes or fold the laundry or mow the lawn.

Please heal sick bodies and wounded hearts. Make those that have given up on ever trusting You again, notice a rainbow and believe there is a promise behind the hues. Help me to shout when life clangs and clatters and whisper when it hurts to break the silence, but to never stop asking You for help. I choose to believe that You care for me and those I love more than any living being ever could. And I will ask again and again and again for miracles, because You want me to.

Amen.

My verse for today:

_____

_____

_____

My prayer:

_____

_____

_____

_____

_____

_____

_____

Prayers #23 Your Presence

When I go to sleep or when I wake, You never leave me. Help me to be conscious of the gentle touch on my shoulder to turn the other way. Help me to listen closely to the whisper in the wind to stop and remember. All the clues of life lead me to You, but they take me strangely through the journeys of other seekers. We are all seeking You, even when we think that there is another way to find life and peace.

Help me to get back up when I think I know better than You. How foolish of me! The fool is one who thinks there is no God. You warn us heavily about that. The fool tries to press against Your way, even while knowing that it is the basis of right and goodness. Teach me to flow along the river of Your righteousness. The current runs swiftly at times and then slows down to a gentle gurgle over rocks and around roots. Interesting, but not without times of rest, I come to You for balance in my life.

Please keep the back and forth of my focus centered on Your Holy Spirit and the leadings that will produce the best outcome for me, and those I love. When my next steps are unclear, shine Your light for me to see the next turn. When I am lost in the woods of indecision, get me back on the trail that leads to home and family and the comfort of a warm blanket with a cup of tea. Thank You for reminding me, again, that You hold my hand to lead the way.

Amen.

My verse for today:

_____
_____
_____

My prayer:

_____
_____
_____
_____
_____
_____
_____

Prayers #24 Your Victory

When the battle between light and darkness clashes in a rage, please point my arrow to make a strike that reaches to the core of corruption. I am often wounded by the spatter coming from those around me. Theirs are stories that tear my heart. Help me to fight the good fight. Help me to recognize the weapons of spiritual warfare. Teach me the lessons of winning in a realm that goes beyond everyday comforts.

It is by Your Holy Spirit that victory is possible. My ways and my wars are not on the strategy table. The battalions are positioned and ready to strike, but I do not see my part. I am but a foot soldier. Help me to respond at once to my Commanding Officer. Help me to see how important it is to be in place when the charge is called. Help me to stand firm and not to falter when the frenzy of conflict beats me down. Help me to trust You when I cannot see the outcome.

When the calm returns after the storm, give me the courage to begin anew. I yield myself to holding the hand of one who has lost those precious parts of a good life. Show me where to head and when to stop and rest a while. Thank You for the green pastures and still waters. I keep needing them along the way.

Amen.

My verse for today:

_____

_____

_____

My prayer:

_____

_____

_____

_____

_____

_____

_____

Prayers #25 Your Names

Blessed be the name of the Lord! Help me to understand the meanings of Your names. You are my Hope in times of discouragement. You are my Comforter when pain comes at me from every direction. You are the Joy of my Salvation; remind me of the gift of new life! You are the Bright and Morning Star that leads my way in darkness and offers a peek into the universe of Your expanse. You are the Way, the Truth, the Life that puts order into a messy world.

Bring me back to a place of total trust and confidence in Your plan and place in my life. I choose to plot all of my decisions around the core of obedience to Your revealed will. Make Truth so clear that I run to it as a deer to water. Expose the lies that seek to confuse and misdirect my attentions so obvious that I laugh at the attempt and turn the other way. Keep me grounded in the Word of Your Covenant that sorts out the rights and wrongs and Who is in charge.

Emmanuel, be with me this day. Healer, make me new as a baby's first breath. God of Peace, teach me to put my weapons down and take the blows from those who have been wounded enough to strike out. Redeemer, I surrender my heart and soul and mind and strength to serve the One who purchased me with that perfect life that chose to come to earth so I could see.

Amen.

My verse for today:

_____
_____
_____

My prayer:

_____
_____
_____
_____
_____
_____
_____

Prayers #26 Your Embrace

You love to surprise me, again and again and again! I never tire of that burst of miracle that takes my breath away at its appearance. Just in time, always perfectly fitting to the need, You brighten the darkest night with true Light!

Please wrap me firmly in the swaddling clothes of the comfort and protection of Your will for me. Keep me from struggling to break free from the bonds of Love. When I am ready, You cut me loose to find my own way, my own faith, not picked out for me from my parents' best. I need always to know You myself. You offer so much grace to seek and search and discover who You really are even when I mock You with my choices and spit on You with my deeds.

A love discovered through hardship is strong. You walked the darkest path to know all my need and pain. You always understand. You promise never to let me go, even when I run away. But when I am ready to turn around and embrace all that You are, I see Your arms open wide and a white robe (made that way by Your own blood), ready for me to slip over my back. We then walk forever, arm in arm, to the goal of the River of Life.

Amen.

My verse for today:

_____

_____

_____

My prayer:

_____

_____

_____

_____

_____

_____

_____

Prayers #27 Your Wisdom

Wisdom calls my name and seeks to know my thoughts. How does God know every hair and still run the universe? Every word of my mouth, my every turn, is recorded in the journals of heaven. I struggle to see You as so big and yet so small to fit deep inside my heart.

My aim today is to hear Your voice a little better, clearer. I know that when that whisper passes by and I obey, it gets a little sharper next time. When I push You away as mere thoughts with which I want not to bother, the distance garbles any messages for me. Obedience and patience are keys to open the door to recognize messages from heaven. I cannot call down the powers from above with bravado. I cannot demand that You bow to my tantrums and fits. When You see that it is perfect timing and I am ready to listen, a single word is more profound than all the volumes read before.

Moses met You in the tent of meeting. Joshua never left his side. I want to cling to You for Wisdom's sake. I want to find the answers to my whys. Peace like a river will show me my way. Teach me to listen for Your voice every day.

Amen.

My verse for today:

_____

_____

_____

My prayer:

_____

_____

_____

_____

_____

_____

_____

Prayers #28 Your Communion

Hello, again! Sometimes I want to hold Your hand and walk along a creek bank, picking wild flowers with the breeze blowing through my hair. Nothing earth shaking. No great crisis. Just a pleasant knowing in my spirit that You will never leave, ever.

Rest can come in the little miracles of finding a routine that flows day by day. Peace envelops me when I learn to accept Your better plan over my plans that sap every ounce of strength. Wisdom walks with me when I embrace her righteousness and simplicity. Even the mountain-shaking Almighty wants to present me with the laws of life written on my heart.

Help me to see Your precepts as principles for daily living, not just as monuments of stone written on some wall. I need to understand the Spirit that breathes life into Your law. I need to surrender my desire for pat formulas that release me from my earnest search for truth. Every day is a new message. Manna rots when we try to store it for weeks on end. Be my Bread of Life and let me feast in communion new every morning

Amen.

My verse for today:

_____

_____

_____

My prayer:

_____

_____

_____

_____

_____

_____

Prayers #29 Your Freedom

Remember when we sat under the stars and listened to the night sounds? Day and night are both alike to You! Darkness is not a scary place. It is just one more expression of Your majesty. The stillness wraps me in a blanket of peace and protection. Nothing can separate me from Your love. You continually promise not to go away.

Help me to turn off the music and the voices and the distractions that occupy my thoughts (so I do not have to view my own sins). Then I realize that the brightness of Your goodness can show my faults, but only so that I confess to freedom. You never taunt me with a lash of "See how far you've fallen."

You cast a line that pulls me to the shore. You scrape away scales from my crusty eyes so truth is real again. Child-like faith believes that miracles happen, people are trying to be good, God sends us father-gifts...

Amen.

My verse for today:

_____

_____

_____

My prayer:

_____

_____

_____

_____

_____

_____

Prayers #30 Your Temple

You told the master craftsmen how to build Your tabernacle. Detailed plans became a solid structure of wood and gold and linen and bronze. Vision became reality. Heaven transported to earth by the voice of God and the hands of people practicing obedience. This was one time Your people got it right. And they celebrated!

Help me to do good deeds and not just dream and pray for You to move someone else. Show me the details I am to construct, my piece of what You are charging Your people to build together today. Help us to flow in harmony, linking arms together to make a strong fortress.

The builders had to make the people stop bringing more and more and more of all they had when You came to visit in the wilderness. If you would just dwell in their midst, life would be a better place. They understood that truth. Help me to view Your presence as such a gift that I can't stop giving all I have to fashion a haven for weary souls.

Amen.

My verse for today:

_____

_____

_____

My prayer:

_____

_____

_____

_____

_____

_____

_____

Prayers #31 Your Glory

A cloud moved Your people long ago. When it stopped, they stopped. When it moved, they moved. Help me to recognize Your glory (character, holiness, creativity, righteousness...) and to follow closely. Help me to see You as You really are, and not to be fooled by the distorted versions portrayed to embitter hearts against You. In truth, You are Goodness and Love. My selfishness twists You into something You are not.

When I really embrace the faith that You exist and are a rewarder of those who diligently seek to find You out, I understand that everything in Your hands can work for good. Lies and pride and evildoers cannot extinguish Your power. You take the scrambled plans that seem lost and broken and make a mosaic that is more beautiful than what came first.

Please direct me to meet someone's need today. If it is just to say hello or to smile while rushing by, let it be with giving-love. Many little things stretched over days and months and years become stepping-stones to a place where hungry hearts come to visit for a while. Take a load off and find a place to rest. I want to build a tent of meeting where others come to see the veil torn in two.

Amen.

My verse for today:

_____

_____

_____

My prayer:

_____

_____

_____

_____

_____

_____

_____

Prayers #32 Your Rest

Thank You for carrying me when I run so fast that tripping is inevitable. I have to remember that being a doer of the Word is more important than being a hearer only. I become frustrated when my prayers are shot off with rocket speed and not a delightful resting place beside the still waters. Help me to find that place of rest when my tendency is to continue bouncing off walls and running in place.

Use me to be kind hands and a warm heart to a cold soul. Melt someone's bitterness through my smile and encouragement. Help me to think more of others than of myself, and all to Your glory and not mine.

You are so faithful to me when I am dead set on my own agenda. I must continue to surrender not only my faults, but also my best qualities to You. Erase my sins, Oh Lord! And use the gifts You have designed in me to fit perfectly into Your Body, the Church. Help all of us to move in symphony, with Your Holy Spirit directing the dance that points all to the glory of our Father, the Almighty, the Great I AM.

Amen.

My verse for today:

_____

_____

_____

My prayer:

_____

_____

_____

_____

_____

_____

Prayers #33 Your Assignment

Help me to read through the boring parts of Your Word. Help me to dig deeply and brush away the sand over the hidden bones of what You have been trying to say for thousands of years. There are nuggets of truth and bits of golden wisdom foreshadowing the coming of the Lamb of God. When I see the fulfillment verses, it helps to see them in context. What a glorious plan of redemption!

Each of us comes to You on a level field, but each of us was designed uniquely with a special place in the tapestry of time. Help me to grasp how that really works. Help me to run to You every day. Teach me to receive Your gifts and favors and blessings. Then show me how to pour out the mixture of all You have given me with all I am permitted to design and create. Let me be excited about the serving of the finished piece. Direct the who and when and where and how I should give it back.

Please give strength to those who are chosen to lead. When they want to run away from the calling, please show them a glimpse of the need as You see it. When the burden is heavy and there is not enough time to complete all the tasks, please sort out the parts to pick up and those to set aside for another day. Bring clarity and reason when all the elements of the calling are shadowed by turmoil. I trust You to be their Leader!

Amen.

My verse for today:

_____

_____

_____

My prayer:

_____

_____

_____

_____

_____

_____

Prayers #34 Your Abundant Life

When I look at other people, I see my sins as in a mirror. Help me to confess my faults to You and not concentrate on another's problems. You can handle them. I just need to worry about me and You. Your ways are so above my ways. Your thoughts are so above my thoughts. Your power is beyond my imagination. You created everything!

There are two ways to look at life. My first response is to see the world with me at the center. Life is for my benefit and purpose and pleasure. The second way is to see You as the hub of the wheel. All of life pours out from You. Your plans are perfect, even when they totally mess with my plans. Until I form the habit of looking at life Your way, I will be continually frustrated and crushed as a pebble under the wheel. Help me to be another spoke that makes the circle round and smooth.

Show me my purpose for today. Help me to surrender tomorrow for another day, not worrying if everyone will bow to my wants. When You spoke of abundant living, You really meant for life to be fun and exciting and full of wonder! Show me how to live that way today. Help me to look at life from Your eyes.

Amen.

My verse for today:

_____

_____

_____

My prayer:

_____

_____

_____

_____

_____

_____

Prayers #35 Your Choice

I am trying harder to see my life Your way. We are such children! If I seek first the kingdom of God, then the other things will be added like a cherry on top. I require such promises just to be good. Then I question why my children make choices that I do not understand. I am programmed with a self-centered heart. The object lesson of life is to voluntarily choose You.

The whole giving-up-my-life-for-You idea has been in the back of my mind, but do I embrace it fully? If I am frustrated, is it because I didn't get my way? Do I trust You to add "all these things" to my protective pot if I give my all away? Is it really true, when I give up my life, You give me a better one? I have seen the other side with my own eyes: keeping my life and possessions and goals to myself only breeds disaster. I want to try harder.

My faith is centered in the belief that Your love and plans and goals for me are even better than I can imagine. Anything short of that takes me back to doing it my way. Anything short of that is just enough faith to make me miserable. I choose to trust You! How many times must I test You and try You before I fully believe? I choose to be inside the circle of Your love. You are my hub. Thank You for such an option!

Amen.

My verse for today:

_____

_____

_____

My prayer:

_____

_____

_____

_____

_____

_____

Prayers #36 Your Second Chance

I love the sound of children's laughter! When they fall down in the snow, they just roll around and then get up again. I need to take some lessons. I need to get back up and do it all again.

Remind me every time I sin in thought or word or deed that I am already forgiven. Blaming someone else will only add one more layer to the grime that covers my head. You have already made atonement. You have already provided the cleansing. I need only to admit it was my fault and then get up and go again.

Freedom comes in many forms, but only one will bring real joy. There is the joyful song in my heart when I am free to be all that I was designed to become. There is dancing and music in my soul when I know that mercy is ready and waiting. There is tenderness and kindness when I have extra forgiveness to pass around. I can be all things to all people because You let me explore the levels of this life and then come openly to You for explanations. The questions do not overwhelm You. The horror of evil does not extinguish Your Light. You are my King; You are my Redeemer; You are my Father and my Lord!

Amen.

My verse for today:

_____

_____

_____

My prayer:

_____

_____

_____

_____

_____

_____

Prayers #37 Your Balance

Fire is warm and bright and burning and frightening, just as water is refreshing and cleansing and powerful and destructive. How can good become evil so quickly? How do I manage to choose right when I am engulf in temptations? How do I live in the truth when I find a deceitful word makes me look better to the world? Please wash away my tendency to stretch reality.

The tug-of-war that pulls at me from across the gulf never stops this side of heaven. I trust that the other side is creative and exciting, but without so much darkness. When I choose (against my own will) Your way, do You send another angel to help on my side of the rope? Entering into Your rest is not so much doing nothing, as much as doing what fits perfectly.

Help me to dance and sing and sweat and labor in Your fields that are harvest white. Show me my rows to dig. Open up the gates meant for me to walk. Help me not to invade someone else's space or try to force them into mine. We all have work to do, but mine is not yours and yours is not mine. Teach me to be at the right place in the right time.

Amen.

My verse for today:

_____

_____

_____

My prayer:

_____

_____

_____

_____

_____

_____

_____

Prayers #38 Your Character

Holy, holy, holy is the Lord God Almighty. Heaven and earth are full of Your glory! When I take the time to honor You for who You are, my eyes are opened a bit more so light shines deep into my soul. You are my Healer, my Provider. You take away the sins of the whole world. You send peace in the midst of chaos. You cover me with the shadow of Your wings.

Thank You for reminding me that when I look Your way my troubles melt like snowflakes on a warm window. You put my life in order. You are my hope that every element of my life is working for some good because You are able to twist the braided strands and make a tapestry.

Bring Your peace to the world and to the heart of one who cries out for kindness and a chance to come out of the hole that keeps getting deeper. When we try to spend our way to happiness, or join one more support group, or meet in places that turn down the lights so no one sees into hollow eyes, send us that little tinkle-bell reminder that Your answer is just around the corner. Help us to take the extra steps to see that Your provision does not charge interest.

Amen.

My verse for today:

_____

_____

_____

My prayer:

_____

_____

_____

_____

_____

_____

Prayers #39 Your Way

My priorities so often need adjusting. Please forgive me for slipping back again and again into routines that I have created that cause stress. Why do I never seem to learn from my mistakes on taking time for the wrong things so the right things suffer? Show me exactly what the right things are for me today.

It all goes back to my way versus Your way in everything from not eating fat to not owing money to giving You my first fruits. There is the constant struggle to wrestle free from swimming upstream in my own pursuits in order to float peacefully along in Your gentle current. Sometimes, even the current of Your way is rapid-like, but that is one more test to see how tightly I can hold on to Your hand.

When Your way seems impossible to navigate, please clear my confused mind and deliver me from the deceiver. I need to remember that adding a little of Your way (for show) does not turn my way into the right course; they are two separate and distinctly different lifestyles. Help me to dig out of trenches that run deep from years of practice. I ask You for a fresh vision of my perfect path.

Amen.

My verse for today:

_____

_____

_____

My prayer:

_____

_____

_____

_____

_____

_____

_____

Prayers #40 Your Love

God is Love. The mathematical formula could read God = Love = Joy = Peace. Love is patient, kind, does not seek its own way, just for starters. Love does not demand that everyone must please me as I insatiably try to please myself. Love does not take, but gives and does not count how much or measure to see if my piece is bigger than your piece. Love <u>does</u> mean saying, "I'm sorry" and then working hard not to go there again.

Dear God! Please renew the truth of what Love means to me and everyone else. That is one area that has gotten trampled in muddy alleys and hung up in gilded palaces with no warmth at all. It has to start with me loving one person at a time. Please reveal the true meaning of Love to me so I can share that experience with someone who has given up hope of finding such a gem.

Please help me to rediscover the simple child-faith that wants to hold Baby Jesus. As a parent, I have faced the heartache of seeing a child so wounded that I would offer myself as a sacrifice. You chose the deepest love-gift when You offered Your one-and-only for the selfish created creatures to torture to the death. I need to see just a flash of Your fingertip and then I will begin to understand.

Amen.

My verse for today:

_____

_____

_____

My prayer:

_____

_____

_____

_____

_____

_____

_____

Printed in the United States
141866LV00004B/1/P